CREATE CODE BASED SAMSUNG GALAXY XCOVER4

create.addsamsunggalaxyxcover4davidgomadza76281 01.start

DAVID GOMADZA

www.twofuture.world

Copyright © 2024 David Gomadza

All rights reserved.

PAPERBACK ISBN: **9798340922373**

DEDICATION

A better future

CONTENTS

CREATE CODE BASED SAMSUNG GALAXY XCOVER4

create.addsamsunggalaxyxcover4davidgomadza7628101.start

Brain-Digital Dicepher- Digital Analogue-Digital Impulses to Brain Action Potentials- Computer/Smartphone- Interface Thoughts to Smartphone/Machine App

ACKNOWLEDGMENTS

Tomorrow's World Order

This book is a continuation of the book titled
Brain-Digital Dicepher-Digital Analogue-Digital Impulses to Brain
Action Potentials-Computer/Smartphone-Interface
Thoughts to Smartphone/Machine App

https://play.google.com/store/books/details/David_Gomadza_Brain_Digital_Dicepher_Digital_Analo?id=_rvrEAAAQBAJ

Therefore read this book as well and apply what is in this book in light of the create code smartphone below

CREATE CODE BASED SAMSUNG GALAXY XCOVER4

create.addsamsunggalaxyxcover4davidgomadza7628101.start

create.   .start
add2386789arto
add386789023asrto
add267890183austuever
add767890283agero
add123487680aerost
adduerstuver
add7213678aserost
add4367812agero
add39678120aserster
add36789024aert
add3867823agererest
add332848136agersuter
add36781838agaroerester
add31467436agester
addauertor
addauerterst
addaertoser
addaerters
addaurter
addasetuver

addagererst
add01234agerst
add234agero
addayuer
addauyer
adduerstuver
adduerstuver
addauyerster
addauyerster
addauyerest
addasetuver
addager
addaererestuver
addrester
adderesteroer
adderesteroer
addaeresteroerst
addauersteruver
addaoperst
addauerestuveroy
addaerest
addasero
addaserosero
addasertoyer
addaserosero
addaserotyer
addaserosturo
addasetuver
addasertyuor
addayer
addaerest
addauyerster
addayeresterester
adderesteroer
addayuerestuerest
addayerestuver
addyerester
addaugererest
addagueresteroyer
addageresteruveroer
addagger

BOOK TITLE

addaggerester
addaggerester
addaggeresteroever
addaggerester
addagerestorer
addsgerourerestor
addaggerestuver
addagerestuverest
addaopter
addagoruyer
addaoererouter
addaoyuerterester
addaopter
addagoster
addagouerestyer
addagouter
adduerstuver
addaggeruvoerest
addaguguger
addagger
addagouer
addagouter
addagger
addasgererest
addasgerereste
addasgererester
addasgereresterest
addagroereret
addagroererete
addagroerereter
addagroerereterest
addagger
addaggere
addaderest
addadereste
addagerest
addagereuster
addagerester
addagerestuver
addagerost
addageresterost

addagereset
addagerestuver
addaotereuver
addasuvserest
addastueverestot
addasutor
addastoper
addasopererest
addasoperestur
addasgerestuver
addasgerestuverester
addaggorerestestuverest
addaomnopqerstuver
addaomnopererest
addaomnoprstover
addaostever
addagoueter
addagoutyoer
addasurer
addaguguerst
addaopergerest
addaerestoper
addageropouer
addaggertyer
addagomner
addgomerety
addgerest
addgerestomnuyer
addaguer
addageretyerestoer
addageromnopergerest
addageromnop
addagersouer
addagoutoer
addaguger
addaguguerestor
addagutugerest
addagouerestgerest
addagerest
addaggerou
addaguterop

BOOK TITLE

addaguguerstoper
addagugugerestuger
addatuguerest
addagerestoter
addagurususteromnop
addauer
addauerest
addauerester
addauguerestrest
addageregost
addaguregerest
addaogerest
addaerestuver
addagerst
addaerest
addagugerest
addasguerest
addaguster
addagugver
addaguverester
addagtuger
addagugyer
addaomner
addaster
addaseter
addasetereter
addauter
addauterest
addauyerester
addauyeresterest
addaggerester
addagerester
addageresturest
addagugerest
addagerestor
addasteresy
addauerest
addaerestuver
addageregerest
addaoger
addaoteruter
addaouer
addaouerest
addaouerestuer

BOOK TITLE

addaouerestuv
addaoterestuger
addaouterestuver
addagerouer
addaguerost
addsgerestuger
addagugutugerest
addaugergerest
addaguerest
addagugergerest
addaougerer
addagutuvger
addagutuger
addagugusuver
addagerest
addagegrsuer
addaggerost
addagugerest
addaguguerest
addaguguerest
addagerestog
addagugertyer
addagugyer
addageryer
addaguoer
addagereyor
addageregerest
addaguerst
addaguyer
addagouver
addaguter
addguger

create.addsamsunggalaxyxcover4davidgomadza7628101.startx84.initialise.now.savex84.start

create.openplaymusicapptouchwithfingertipandopenplaymusicthenchooseplayelectromangeticwavecleanermp3=02898678.startx84.initialise.now.savex84.start
create.key1=02898678.start
create.playkey1.start
create.keyinphonenumber07719210295anddialthenumber=key2=0898683867.startx84.initialise.now.savex84.start
create.playkey2.start

BOOK TITLE

KEYS AND FUNCTIONS

KEY1 playelectromagneticwavercleaner
KEY2 checkfortransenders
KEY3 0898286 poweron
KEY4 062890(2077) enterpin
KEY5 0892684 swipescreentoenterpincode
KEY6 0868283 enterpincode2077andpressok
KEY7 0828728 openphonedial
KEY8 0898386 openkeypad
KEY9 08286386 dial0784262990andcall
KEY10 08284810 clickrecent
KEY11 08284811 clickcontacts
KEY12 08284812 clickplaces
KEY13 08284813 pressreturnbutton
KEY14 08284814 clicktoopenmessages
KEY15 08284815 clickmessagesicontocompose
KEY16 08284816 clickrecipientandenterphonenumber
KEY17 08284817 ifscreenlockcomesonpresspowerbutton
KEY18 08284818 thenswipescreentoenterpin
KEY19 08284819 enterpincode2077andpressok
KEY20 08284820 click messagebox
KEY21 08284821 typemessage
KEY22 08284822 clicksendmessagebutton
KEY23 08284823 clicktoopencamera
KEY24 08284824 clicktoswitchtobackcamera
KEY25 08284825 clicktoswitchtofrontcamera
KEY26 08284826 clickshutterbuttonandtakeyourself
KEY27 08284824 clickflipbuttontoswitchtobackcamera
KEY27 08284826 clickshutterbuttonandtakewhatsinfrontofyou
KEY29 08284813 pressreturnbuttontoexitcamera
KEY30 08284827 clicktoopencalculator
KEY31 08284828
sayinternalcalculatormultiplysubtractdivideaddallnumbetsandgiveanswer

BOOK TITLE

verbally.start
KEY32 08284813 pressreturnbuttontoexitcalculator
KEY34 08284829 clickplaymusic
KEY35 08284830 playcurrenttrack
KEY36 08284831 stopplaycurrenttrack
KEY37 08284832 clickshuffleall
KEY38 08284833 pressreturnbuttonseveraltimestoexitfully
KEY39 08284834 clicktoopenvoicerecorder
KEY40 08284835 pressredbuttontostartrecording
KEY41 08284836 pressredstopbuttontostoprecording
KEY42 08284837 pressoktosavetherecording
KEY43 08284838 pressplaybuttontoplaytherecording
KEY44 08284839 pressstopbuttontostoptherecording
KEY45 08284840 pressreturnbuttontoexit
KEY46 08284841 doyouwanttoexitapppressoktoexitvoicerecorder
KEY47 08284842 presspoweroffbutton

RECAP EXTRACTS FROM:
Brain-Digital Dicepher-
Digital Analogue-Digital
Impulses to Brain Action
Potentials-
Computer/Smartphone-
Interface
Thoughts to
Smartphone/Machine App

Brain-Digital Dicepher-
Digital Analogue-Digital
Impulses to Brain Action
Potentials-
Computer/Smartphone-
Interface
Thoughts to
Smartphone/Machine App
INTRODUCTION
We can operate any smartphone, computer or laptop using our brain thoughts. Yes we can simply think of a number like 33 on a Samsung galaxy s22 Ultra to dial a number and make a phone call. Or we can simply think of a number 4 and open google on our smartphone Samsung galaxy s22 ultra . We can think of a number like 54 to open

a further app like Natural God Intelligence and ask any question we want. This is possible now. I decoded the brain and invented a decipher that calculates codes we can use to open any app or function on a Samsung galaxy s22 ultra.

Every app in any smartphone has a code. Opening the app has a code and this action of opening the app has a code that is linked to a corresponding brain action potential and a brain impulse code.

That means the message app on a Samsung galaxy s22 ultra is known by code 28 and a brain impulse of 74 and a brain action potential of 97.

That means we just need to think the number 74 to open.

To open the app you simply need to think the brain action potential first which is 97. This number is sent to the brain action potential sockets. In the sockets the number is converted into binary and the correct is assigned. This is then sent to the brain impulse sockets where it is fed into the sockets. It is broken down from binary and another value is added to make sure it fits into the next sockets namely that of corresponding brain impulses.

Now we need to write that if brain action potential is the same as the brain impulse then we can get a value we can use to find the corresponding responds from the central nervous system.

We can then ask two questions.

1. What are the values we need to make sure that if a person thinks then what happens is what he could simply have done by his hand.

2. That means if one thinks he is imply substituting the hand actions with a thinking code but one that does exactly the same.

Now we can get the value by a simply equation that says if $x=y$ then y and x must be related somehow.

That means if we are to take x and substitute it with y we can get the same results.

x and y are the values we must first get to complete the action.

In the example above where we want to open messages just by thinking we can simply give the brain action potential value first that is 97.

97 is the same as 74 which is the corresponding value but a brain impulse rather than a brain action potential.

If we substitute the first with the second we can make the brain acts as if the hand is the one that has clicked the app and opened it.

The brain can do this by a series of commands that will culminate

with the opening of the app just from a simply thought of that action

rather than the actual opening of the app.

The steps the brain takes to replace the thinking with the actual opening of the app using a code in this case code 74.

First the brain must ask itself if the message can be easily decoded without the need for other databases etc.

The brain then moves on to the actual carrying out of such a task by substituting the action potential of 97 with the brain impulse of 74. That means that the brain has converted the body action potential you would get if the hand had clicked the message app. That means opening the app and giving this process a number corresponding to the person 76 for a man and 71 for a woman.

That means the person is linked to his actions as people are different what a person who is short can do is different to what a person who is tall can do that means the number must be linked to the person.

Now the brain will ask itself if the rules are met that is if the person has followed what the body would normally do in that circumstance.

Now the brain is ready to execute the action.

The brain will move the app itself in its mind [mind of the brain]. Now we can assume that the brain has a hand which it will move just as the person will. It then records all the possible movements and records all this. It gives each segment of the move a code linked to the person and one to itself.

It then asks itself what has been moved and records this. Now when we simply input the code which is a brain impulse it will now simply replace all the sequence with a code it has recorded.

Now it will simply input the code into the new sockets it has created. Every time the brain creates a new movement it creates sockets that can be easily used to shorten things and make the repeating of this move possible through these sockets.

We can simply ask the brain to insert a value into the socket and decode what the number is. This is what it uses to create a brain decipher.

This is a complex instrument like thing that it uses to just get a code and input it to know exactly what is the corresponding brain impulse. Now you can easily pick a number using the example above 28 This decipher can easily find out the corresponding brain impulse of 74. It can then use this brain impulse value to find a corresponding brain action potential.

Now we can easily say that whatever happens in life is guarded by what the body has as numbers. Once the body has assigned value to tasks and actions forever it will use these to carry out tasks above all will try to reduce the time it takes and how the task is carried out. Over a long period od time these numbers becomes part of the brain. Now all it has to do is to create a template like with all numbers it uses.

These numbers will forever be part of you and the brain and in most cases the numbers will be specific to an individual. Let us take for example the number 8 that is often associated with Yahweh or God.

Yahweh is the almighty

Yahweh never sleeps

Yahweh can hear all

Yahweh has power

Yahweh is everlasting

Yahweh the merciful

Yahweh the only king and ruler

Yahweh how come I am here before my time

Yahweh I am who I am

Yahweh is God

Yahweh is high

Yahweh is omnipotent

Yahweh is omnipresent

Yahweh is the omniscience

All these are all of value 8 the brain need just to pick the correct context to assign a value and a digit.

That means we must also create a decoder that tells us the context as well we must also assign a value for the other values we might encounter but ones we are not aware of.

We must ask people some questions to get a likely response which we can then use to come up with a way of assigning the correct context to any situation.

We must therefore create another digital decoder which identifies

1. The asker

2. The decoder

3. The environment surrounding the question..

Read the above book.

Visit www.twofuture.world

www.ingramcontent.com/pod-product-compliance
Lightning Source LLC
Chambersburg PA
CBHW071002220526
45471CB00007B/3135